There are five sleepy bats hanging around in this book. Can you find them?

my HUMAN BODY Infographic sticker Activity BOOK

WAYLAND
www.waylandbooks.co.uk

Activity stickers, and extra ones to use anywhere in the book, can be found at the back.

BRAIN

Uses 20 per cent of your energy, but is just 2 per cent of your body's weight.

EARS

Help you keep balance, and hear sound.

HEART

Beats 100,000 times a day.

STOMACH

Food stays in your stomach for

EYES

Send more information to your brain than your other four senses — hearing, smell, taste and touch — added together.

NOSE

A sneeze travels at 160 kilometres per hour. That is as fast as a racing car!

MOUTH

You are born with about 10,000 taste buds on your tongue.

LUNGS

You breathe 11,000 litres of air every day.

MUSCLES

You have 640 muscles in your body.

BONES

Bones are stronger than steel.

INTESTINES (in-TEST-ins)

Long tubes that help break down food. When you are fully grown, they will be about 7 metres long.

YOUR BRILLIANT BODY

Even though you look different to everyone else, your body has the same parts as they do. These parts work together to keep you alive.

FUNNY BONES

Your skeleton is a strong, light, bendy frame made of bone that gives your body its shape. Bones also protect some parts of you. Your skull protects your brain, and your ribs protect your lungs and your heart.

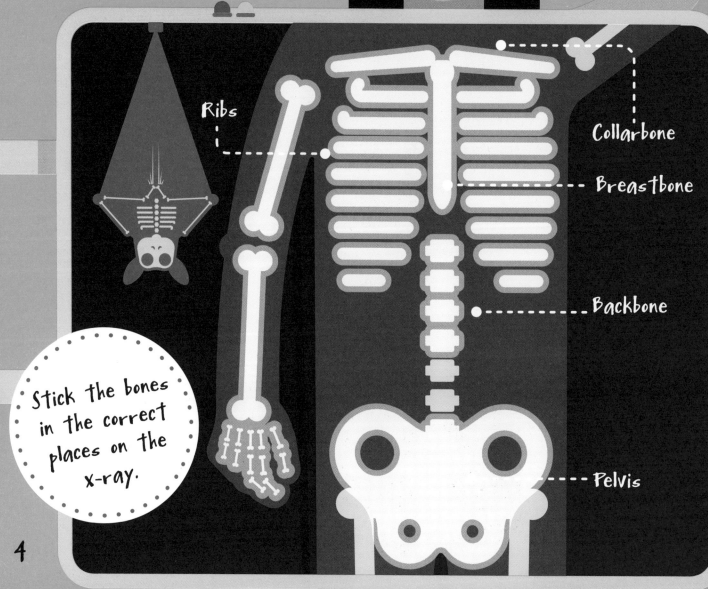

Ribs

Collarbone

Breastbone

Backbone

Pelvis

Stick the bones in the correct places on the x-ray.

Bone is very strong. A cube of bone can support 8,618 kilograms before it cracks. That is about the same as five cars!

Stick three cars on the cube of bone.

Actual size

2.5 cm

Compact bone

Bone marrow

Spongy bone

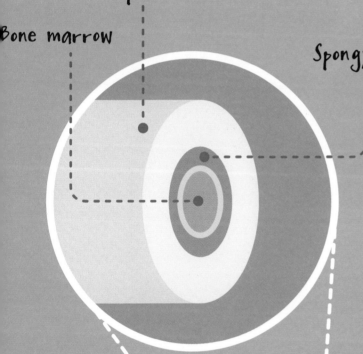

Your bones are not solid. A layer of softer 'spongy' bone goes around the marrow and this is surrounded by harder 'compact' bone.

Add the marrow to the middle of the bone.

MUSCLE POWER

Muscles are a lot like elastic — they stretch and relax so that you can move your body. The muscles in your arms help you lift and carry things, the ones in your legs help you walk and run. The muscles in your face help you smile and frown.

The heaviest weight a person has ever lifted above their head is 263 kilograms. That is about the same as three kangaroos.

Stick in the two kangaroos.

Stick these mighty muscles on the podium and add the medals.

The muscles around your eye are the strongest, for their size.

Your heart is your hardest-working muscle — it starts working before you are born and never takes a break.

You are probably sitting on the largest muscle in your body — your bottom!

STRONGEST

BUSIEST

BIGGEST

THE SKIN YOU ARE IN

Skin is like a 'living coat' that protects your insides from the outside world.

Your skin makes something called melanin (MEL-a-nin), which gives skin its colour and helps protect you from the S

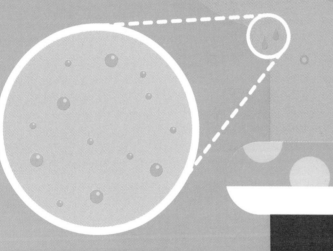

Your skin is waterproof.

If you get hot your skin sweats to cool it down.

Stick a sur and rain clo in the sky

If your skin gets hurt it starts to repair itself straight away.

Put a plaster on the cut to help keep out germs.

No one has exactly the same fingerprints as you — even identical twins have different fingerprints. There are three main types of fingerprint pattern: the whorl, the arch and the loop.

whorl

arch

loop

Put some ink on your thumb and make your own print in the thumb space. Can you tell which type of print you have? Get someone else to do a print of their little finger in the other space. How is it different from yours?

HAIR WE GO!

Hair grows all over your body but you probably only notice the longer, thicker stuff that grows on your head. Head hair is very strong. A whole head of hair could support 12 tonnes, that is the same as three hippos.

Stick the hippos dangling from the hair.

You have the same number of hairs on your body as a chimpanzee! The only difference is that the hair on a chimpanzee's body is long and thick, but the hair on your body is short and fine.

SUPER COMPUTER

You brain is like a powerful computer. It lets you feel, move and think. It also controls things inside of your body that you do not notice. Different parts of your brain do different jobs.

thinking

moving

speaking

reading

touching

hearing

remembering

seeing

Stick the different jobs in the correct part of the brain.

Nerves are like cables that carry messages backwards and forwards between your brain and other parts of your body. These messages travel along your nerves at about 400 kilometres per hour. That is nearly as fast as the Shanghai Maglev — the world's fastest train.

I'm off to tell the brain that this pin prick is painful!

Stick the super-fast train next to the nerve.

13

SWEET DREAMS

We all need to sleep because it gives your body time to grow. Babies need the most sleep — about 16 hours a day — because they grow so quickly. When you have finished growing you will only need about eight hours of sleep a day.

Stick 11 clocks above the bed so this child gets a good night's sleep.

= 1 hour

Colour in the duvet cover.

All living creatures need sleep, but some snooze in mysterious ways ...

Bats sleep upside down.

Stick these animals in your book so they can have a rest.

Dolphins sleep with one eye open — only half of their brain sleeps at a time.

Horses can sleep standing up.

Colour in this dolphin.

SEE HEAR ...

Your eyes let you see. Light goes into your eye through the small black hole in the middle, called the 'pupil'. Messages then travel from your eye to your brain, which makes sense of what you are looking at.

EYELASHES

Helps to stop dust and grit getting into your eye.

IRIS

The coloured p of the eye.

PUPIL

The black hole in the middle of your eye that lets in light.

EYELID

You need your eyelids to blink. Blinking spreads tears across your eye to keep it clean and stop it drying out.

Stick the pupi in the middle o the eye. Colour i the iris. Which colour will you choose?

Your ear 'catches' sounds from the air and sends them into the hidden part of your ear inside of your head. This is where you will find your eardrum — a piece of skin that moves backwards and forwards when sounds hit it.

actual size!

This is where you will also find the stirrup bone — the smallest bone in your body.

Stick the bones inside of the ear.

PERFECT PUMP

Your heart is a special muscle that pumps blood around your body. It beats about 100,000 times and pumps about 7,200 litres of blood every day — over a lifetime, that is enough to fill half a supertanker

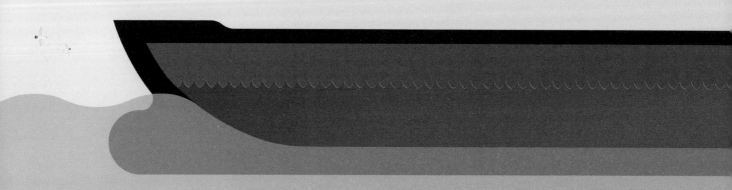

BLUE WHALE
10 beats
per minute

HORSE
40 beats
per minute

HUMAN
70 beats
per minute

DOG
80 beats
per minute

You don't have enough stickers for me! A hummingbird's heart beats at 1,260 beats per minute.

 = 10 beats per minute

Use your stickers to show how many times these animals' hearts beat in one minute.

The average human heart beats about 70 times per minute. It gets faster if you are exercising or nervous. But not all animals' hearts beat at the same speed.

TAKE A DEEP BREATH

Your lungs are like two big sponges that hold air instead of water. When you breathe in, air gets sucked into your lungs and travels down tubes. At the end of the smallest tubes are tiny bags called alveoli (al-VEE-oh-lie) that look like bunches of grapes. This is where the air you breathe begins its journey round your body.

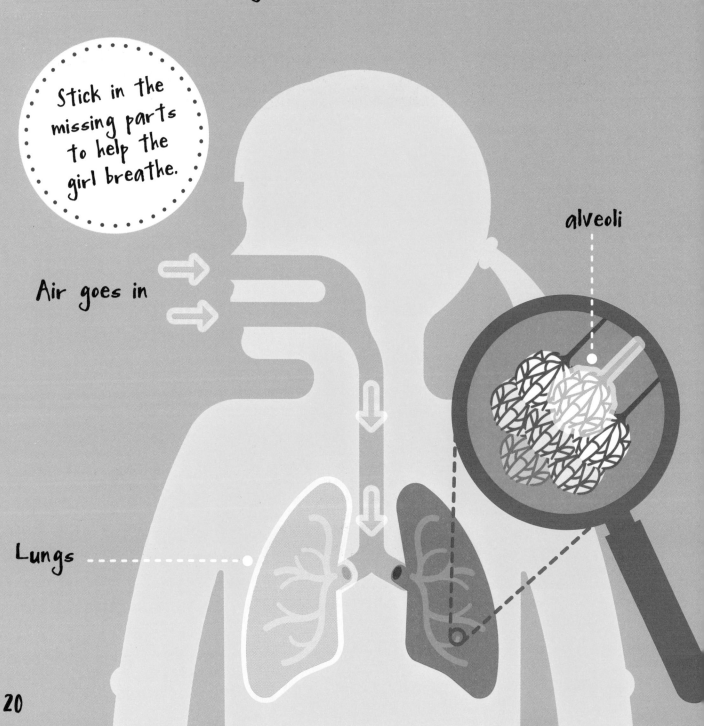

Stick in the missing parts to help the girl breathe.

Air goes in

alveoli

Lungs

You can probably hold your breath for about a minute. Some divers can hold their breath for as long as 20 minutes. But some animals can hold their breath for much longer.

DIVER
20 minutes

EMPEROR PENGUIN
20 minutes

SEA LION
60 minutes

SPERM WHALE
90 minutes

ELEPHANT SEAL
2 hours

EEN SEA
URTLE
7 hours

Stick the animals in the ocean. Give medals to the three animals that can hold their breath for the longest.

SAY 'AAAAH!'

Bitter tastes

Your tongue is covered with lots of tiny bumps called tastebuds. These work out what flavour the food or drink is that you are enjoying.

Stick the different flavours of food on to the tongue.

Salty tastes

Sour tastes

Give the narwhal his tooth back by sticking it in the book.

Savoury tastes

When you are young you have 20 'milk' teeth which start to fall out when you are five or six years old.

Sweet tastes

The most unusual tooth belongs to the narwhal. The male's horn is actually a tooth which grows up to 2.7 metres long.

FOOD FOR THOUGHT

Food goes on an interesting journey after you've eaten it.
Follow the sandwich to see what happens ...

1. MOUTH

Teeth crush and mash food, spit helps to make it soft.

2. OESOPHAGUS ('EE-soff-a-gus')

After food is swallowed, it slips into a tube that leads to your stomach.

3. STOMACH

Food is churned up, a bit like cement in a cement mixer, until it turns into a soupy liqu

4. SMALL INTESTINE

This long twisty tube is where t goodness is tak out of food so i can be used by your body.

5. LARGE INTESTINE

The bits of foo you cannot use travel through this shorter, wider tube on the way out your body...

Feed the child a sandwich and use the arrow stickers to show its journey through the body.

EXIT

You will probably chomp your way through 27 tonnes of food over your whole lifetime. That is about the same as eating three T-rexs!

Colour in the hungry T-rex.

I think I will need a bigger plate ...

BABY STEPS

It takes nearly nine months for a human baby to grow.

Use your stickers to see how the growing baby changes.

At five weeks, it is as big as an apple pip.

At eight weeks, it is the same size as a strawberry

Some animal babies grow quickly, others take much longer...

ELEPHANT
2 years

GORILLA
8.5 months

At 24 weeks, it is about as long as an ear of corn.

At 12 weeks, it is as big as a mouse.

At 38 weeks, the baby is fully grown.

These animal babies are nearly ready to be born. Find their mum and stick them in her tummy.

HUMAN
9 months

CAT
2 months

HAMSTER
2 weeks

TALL TALE, SHORT STORY

Girls and boys are about the same height. Grown men are usually taller than women. But some people are much taller, or smaller, than this ...

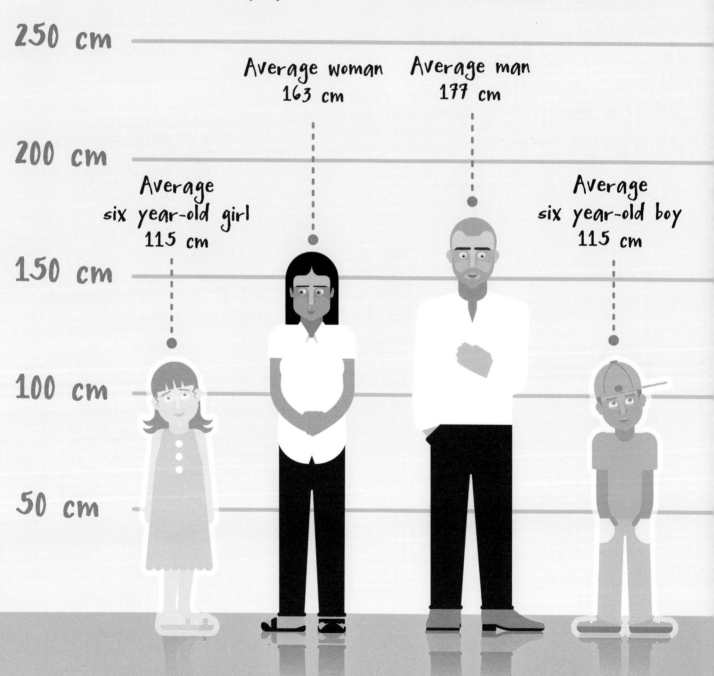

250 cm

Average woman
163 cm

Average man
177 cm

200 cm

Average
six year-old girl
115 cm

Average
six year-old boy
115 cm

150 cm

100 cm

50 cm

In the first year of their life, babies grow the fastest. After the age of 2, children grow about 5–6 centimetres every year, and then they grow quickly again as teenagers. People stop growing at about 20 years old.

My shoe is 47 cm long. That is almost as tall as Chandra!

Tallest person ever was Robert Pershing Wadlow 272 cm

rtest person ever was
andra Bahadur Dangi
54.6 cm

Robert was as tall as 12 footballs stacked on top of each other.

Stick the people and footballs on to the height chart to see how tall they are.

ANIMAL OLYMPICS

You can run, swim, jump and lift — but humans are no match for these awesome animals ...

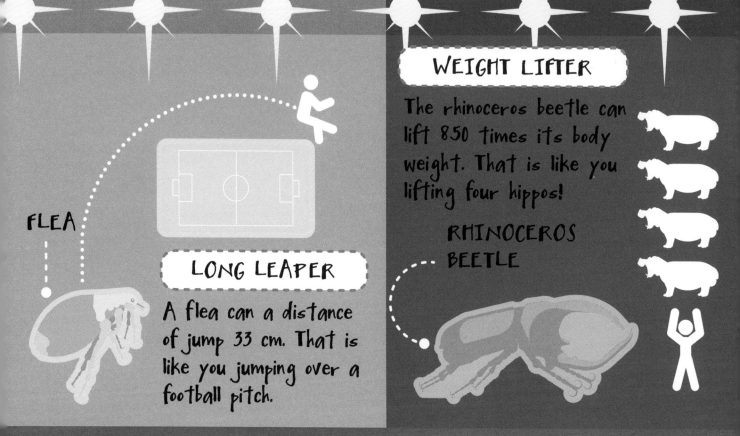

WEIGHT LIFTER

The rhinoceros beetle can lift 850 times its body weight. That is like you lifting four hippos!

RHINOCEROS BEETLE

FLEA

LONG LEAPER

A flea can a distance of jump 33 cm. That is like you jumping over a football pitch.

FAST RUNNER

The fastest animal on land is the cheetah, who can run at 110 kilometres per hour. That is more than twice the speed of the fastest human.

HUSKEY

Catch me if you can.

Weeee!

HIGH JUMPER

A tiny bug called a froghopper can jump 70 cm in the air. That is like a person jumping over two Big Ben clock-towers.

SAILFISH

FROGHOPPER

QUICK SWIMMER

he sailfish can reach speeds of 110 ilometres per hour. That is about 12 mes faster than the fastest human.

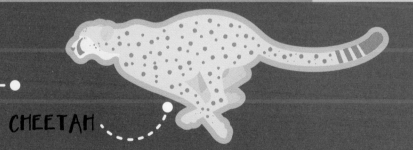

CHEETAH

LONG-DISTANCE LEGEND

But, when it comes to running big distances over a long time, humans are pretty good. This is because we only need two legs to run, and we can eat and drink while on the move. Only huskies can keep up.

PUZZLE ANSWERS

Did you find all of the bats? If you did not spot them all, here is where they were hiding ...

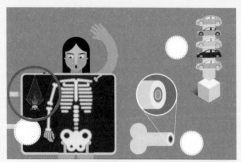

Pages 4–5

Pages 6–7

Pages 10–1[...]

Pages 14–15

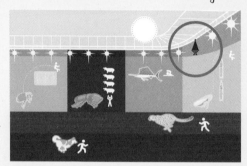

Pages 30–31

First published in 2016 by Wayland
© Wayland 2016
All rights reserved.
Written by Jo Dearden
Edited by Corinne Lucas
Illustration and design by Wild Pixel Ltd.
ISBN: 978 0 7502 9942 8
Printed in Malaysia
10 9 8 7 6 5 4 3 2 1

Wayland, an imprint of Hachette Children's Group
Part of Hodder & Stoughton
Carmelite House
50 Victoria Embankment
London, EC4Y 0DZ
www.hachette.co.uk
www.hachettechildrens.co.uk

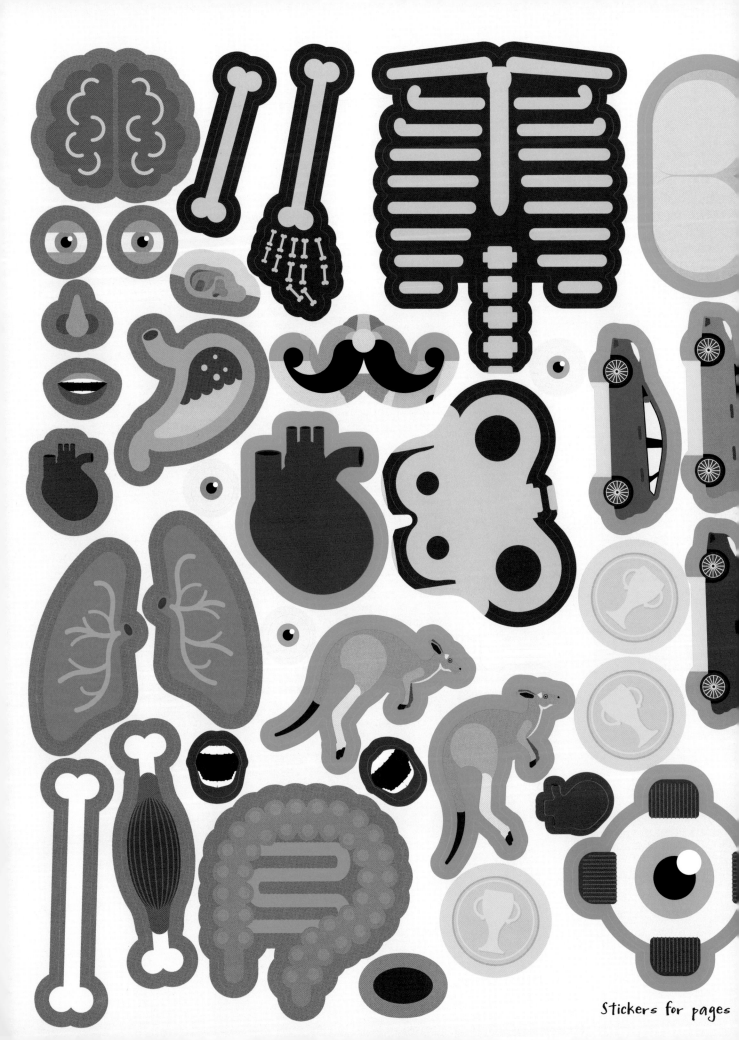

Stickers for pages 26–31.